W9-AKD-930

755

Min

Miniature Schnauzers
and Other Terriers

Editorial:
Editor in Chief: Paul A. Kobasa
Project Manager: Cassie Mayer
Senior Editor: Christine Sullivan
Writer: Ana Deboo
Researcher: Cheryl Graham
Manager, Contracts & Compliance
  (Rights & Permissions): Loranne K. Shields
Indexer: David Pofelski

Graphics and Design:
Manager: Tom Evans
Coordinator, Design Development
  and Production: Brenda B. Tropinski
Contributing Photographs Editor: Clover Morell
Cartographer: John Rejba

Pre-Press and Manufacturing:
Director: Carma Fazio
Manufacturing Manager:
  Steven K. Hueppchen
Production/Technology Manager:
  Anne Fritzinger

For information about other World Book publications,
visit our Web site at http://www.worldbookonline.com
or call 1-800-WORLDBK (967-5325).

For information about sales to schools and libraries,
call 1-800-975-3250 (United States),
or 1-800-837-5365 (Canada).

World Book, Inc.
233 N. Michigan Avenue
Chicago, IL 60601
U.S.A.

Library of Congress Cataloging-in-Publication Data
Miniature schnauzers and other terriers.
    p. cm. -- (World Book's animals of the world)
    Includes index.
    Summary: "An introduction to miniature schnauzers
and other terriers, presented in a highly illustrated,
question-and-answer format. Features include fun
facts, glossary, resource list, index, and scientific
classification list"--Provided by publisher.
    ISBN 978-0-7166-1366-4
    1. Terriers--Juvenile literature. 2. Miniature schnauzer--
Juvenile literature. I. World Book, Inc.
SF429.T3M56 2010
636.755--dc22
                                        2009020167
World Book's Animals of the World
Set 6: ISBN: 978-0-7166-1365-7
Printed in China by Leo Paper Products LTD., Heshan, Guangdong
1st printing November 2009

Picture Acknowledgments: Cover: © Mark Raycroft, Minden Pictures; © BaileyOne/Shutterstock;
© Natalia V Guseva, Shutterstock; © Claudia Steininger, Dreamstime; © Linda Bearden.

© Arco Images GmbH/Alamy Images 15, 17; © Juniors Bildarchiv/Alamy Images 61; © Design Pics/Alamy
Images 35; © Lynn Hilton, Alamy Images 59; © Idamini/Alamy Images 19; © Mary Evans Picture
Library/Alamy Images 9; © tbkmedia/Alamy Images 11; © TongRo Image Stock/Alamy Images 55;
© Petra Wegner, Alamy Images 25; © Linda Bearden 43; © Alison Bowden, Dreamstime 33;
© Ispace/Dreamstime 51; © Pixbilder/Dreamstime 37; © Claudia Steininger, Dreamstime 45;
© Fotolia 27; © Timothy A. Clary, AFP/Getty Images 29; © Mariusz Forecki, AFP/Getty Images 53;
© Vikki Hart, Getty Images 31; © Colin Hawkins, Getty Images 41; © Mark Raycroft, Minden Pictures 7, 49;
© Michelle D. Bridwell, PhotoEdit 23; © Shutterstock 3, 4, 5, 21, 39, 47, 57.

Illustrations: WORLD BOOK illustration by Roberta Polfus 13.

World Book's Animals of the World

Miniature Schnauzers
and Other Terriers

WORLD
BOOK

a Scott Fetzer company
Chicago
www.worldbookonline.com

Contents

What Is a Terrier?

Terriers *(TEHR ee uhrz)* are dogs that were originally bred to chase and hunt such animals as rabbits, brown rats, or foxes. These animals often live in burrows—holes and tunnels in the ground used as homes. The word *terrier* came from the Latin word *terra,* which meant "earth." Terriers got this name because they often dug in the ground to catch their prey (animals they hunt).

Since part of their job was to kill burrowing animals, early terriers were often aggressive, or ready to get in a fight. A few terriers were even used in dog fighting. These events, in which people watched animals fight, became illegal in most places during the 1800's, as people came to realize how cruel the sport was for the animals.

By the late 1800's, people were breeding terriers to be friendly companions instead of fighters. A hint of their old aggressiveness still remains, though. Most terriers are energetic and vocal, eager to run around and bark to defend their family.

A miniature schnauzer

How Did Breeds of Terriers Develop?

A breed is a group of animals that has the same type of ancestors. When people breed dogs, they choose parents that have the particular talents and traits (features or characteristics) they want the puppies to have. In the case of terriers, the usual goal was to breed dogs that would help keep people's living areas free of vermin—animals that are considered by many to be troublesome or destructive. Vermin might include rats and rabbits. Other terriers were bred to chase larger animals, such as foxes or badgers.

The looks of the different terrier breeds hint at the kind of job for which the dog was originally bred. Many terriers are small and have short legs, which made it easier for them to follow vermin into cramped burrows. Terriers with longer legs were better at chasing larger, faster animals. Most terriers, whatever their size, have coarse (rough) coats that easily shed dirt.

LEIGHTON, BROS.

THE RAT HOLE.

By "ARMFIELD."

Small terriers were bred to hunt such animals as rats.

9

When and Where Did the Miniature Schnauzer Breed First Appear?

The miniature schnauzer *(SHNOW zuhr)* was developed in Germany in the 1800's. The word *miniature* means small. The word *schnauzer* comes from a word that means "snout" in German. An animal's snout is the part of the head that extends forward and contains the nose, mouth, and jaws. Perhaps the schnauzer got its name because its snout, with its distinctive "beard," was so noticeable.

The miniature schnauzer was created in Germany by crossing the standard schnauzer, a larger version of the schnauzer, with several smaller types of dogs. One of these smaller dogs was a toy breed, the affenpinscher *(AH fuhn PIHN shuhr).* The tiny affenpinscher was originally bred to kill rats.

The miniature schnauzer was introduced as a breed in Germany in 1899. In 1926, the American Kennel Club (AKC), the major registry of purebred dogs in the United States, recognized the miniature schnauzer.

North
America

Asia

Germany

Atlantic
Ocean

Europe

Africa

Equator

Map showing Germany, the
country where the miniature
schnauzer developed

An affenpinscher

11

What Does a Miniature Schnauzer Look Like?

The miniature schnauzer is a small, sturdy dog that is ideally around 13 inches (33 centimeters) tall at the shoulder. It was bred to be a smaller version of the standard schnauzer, which is ideally around 19 inches (48 centimeters) tall at the shoulder. Like the standard schnauzer, the miniature schnauzer has fur on its face that looks like bushy eyebrows and a beard. The traditional colors for its wiry coat are solid black, black streaked with silver, or salt-and-pepper gray, but breeders have produced other colors as well.

Some people crop schnauzers' ears—that is, they have them trimmed to make them stand up. Long ago, this was thought to protect the dog's ears from the sharp claws of its prey. Now ear cropping is by choice, even for show dogs. Some people also dock (cut short) the dog's tail. Naturally, the miniature schnauzer would have a fairly short, thin tail. When docked, the tail would be a small stub. Many pet owners choose to leave the dog's natural tail. In some countries, ear cropping and tail docking are not allowed.

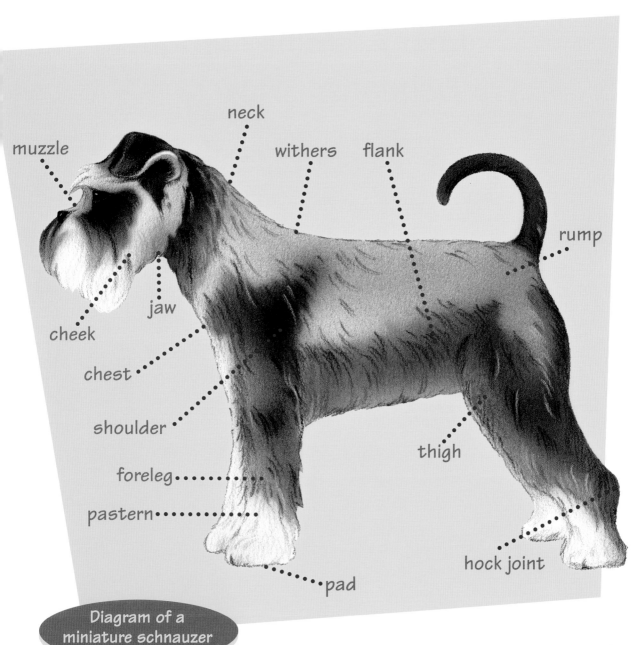

muzzle

neck

withers

flank

rump

jaw

cheek

chest

shoulder

thigh

foreleg

pastern

hock joint

pad

Diagram of a
miniature schnauzer

13

What Kind of Personality Might a Miniature Schnauzer Have?

The miniature schnauzer is a popular dog breed, and one reason is because of its lively nature. Of course, every dog is different, and dogs that have been badly treated or that were bred from parents with poor personalities are less likely to match the ideal. But under good circumstances, miniature schnauzers are smart, eager to learn, and obedient. They tend to be friendly—but cautious—with everyone they meet, whether people or other dogs. They especially like to play with their family.

Like other terriers, miniature schnauzers are usually bold dogs with lots of energy. These traits can lead to problems if a dog is not properly trained.

Miniature schnauzers can be cautious dogs.

Is a Miniature Schnauzer the Dog for You?

The small size of the miniature schnauzer might make the breed a good choice for people who live in an apartment. But miniature schnauzers are energetic dogs that need a fair amount of exercise. Even families who have a fenced yard will still need to take such an energetic dog as this on walks. And if a barking dog will cause problems with neighbors, a quieter breed might be a better choice.

The American Kennel Club (AKC) recognizes more than 150 dog breeds, and there are also many kinds of mixed-breed dogs. People who want a dog that is right for them can usually find one.

For many people, the miniature schnauzer is a fine choice for a pet. These dogs love their families, they usually do well with other pets, and they are smart, playful, and fun. And because schnauzers do not shed much, they are less likely to bother people with allergies.

Miniature schnauzers need much exercise.

17

What Should You Look for When Choosing a Miniature Schnauzer Puppy?

Before deciding to get a puppy, think about what is involved. Your dog may live as long as 14 years, or longer. Can you take care of a pet for its entire life? Further, you or someone in your family will need to train the dog.

Responsibility is a job or task you promise to do. A puppy is a big responsibility, but if you think you can handle it, you might begin to research different breeds by talking to a veterinarian or other dog owners. The Internet also has much information on specific breeds. (See the Web sites listed on page 64 of this book.)

Once you have decided on a miniature schnauzer puppy, you will need to find a good breeder. It takes skill to select parent dogs and to care for newborn puppies. A breeder's good work ensures that your puppy is healthy and happy when it comes to live with you.

A miniature
schnauzer puppy

Should You Get an Older Miniature Schnauzer Instead of a Puppy?

A puppy is not for everyone. If you cannot give a puppy the time and training it needs, an older dog might be a better choice for you and your family. Grown dogs still require time, training, and love, but they are usually a lot less work than a puppy.

A grown dog of most breeds, including the miniature schnauzer, will ordinarily be calmer than a puppy. A grown dog you choose should already be housebroken (trained to relieve itself outside of the house). Many older dogs may also be trained for basic things, such as walking on a leash.

An older dog may adjust to your home routines more easily, and it will not get as lonely when you have to be away for a short while. A grown dog might take a bit longer to form an emotional bond with you than a puppy would, but this will usually still happen.

20

An older miniature schnauzer

What Does a Miniature Schnauzer Eat?

Like all dogs, miniature schnauzers need to eat a proper diet to stay healthy. Dogs need different nutrients, or nourishing things, than people do. That's why dogs do better when they are fed dog food rather than table scraps (human food).

Your veterinarian can advise you about the best kinds of prepared dry or wet dog food to give your miniature schnauzer. Be sure that fresh water is always available.

Many experts think pets should never eat human foods, while others feel occasional treats are okay. Certain foods, however, can harm or even kill a dog, including chocolate, grapes, raisins, soft drinks, and sugarless candies. Do not feed your pet anything unless you know it is safe.

Miniature schnauzer puppies eating

25

Where Should a Miniature Schnauzer Sleep?

Miniature schnauzers are small dogs that often enjoy cuddling with their human owners, so it may be tempting to let yours sleep in bed with you. It is probably better, though, to teach your dog to sleep in its own place. This might be in a specially designed dog bed, on a cozy blanket, or in a carrier crate positioned in a quiet spot.

The advantage to this is that the dog can establish a bedtime routine—that is, doing the same thing every night. It will have a place that will help it feel safe even when you have to be away from home. Also, some dogs are not very good at sharing a bed, and your pet may make it hard for you to sleep.

26

A miniature schnauzer in a cozy dog bed

How Do You Groom a Miniature Schnauzer?

Most dogs need to have their coat groomed. Many terriers, including schnauzers, have an unusual coat. They have both longer fur and very short fur known as an undercoat.

To look its best, a schnauzer needs a special haircut. Many people let a professional groomer do this about every two months. Usually, a groomer uses clippers to trim a schnauzer's fur. The fur is left longer on the ears, legs, and chest. Longer fur is also left above the dog's eyes, on the nose, and for the "beard" on its muzzle.

In between haircuts, brush a miniature schnauzer at least twice a week. Brushing a dog is good for its skin, prevents tangles, and makes its coat shiny.

Bathe your dog when necessary, but don't bathe it too often. Dogs have important oils on their skin that can be stripped away with overbathing.

Trim your dog's nails about every two weeks. Some people ask their groomer to cut the nails, but your vet can show your parent or guardian the proper way to clip them.

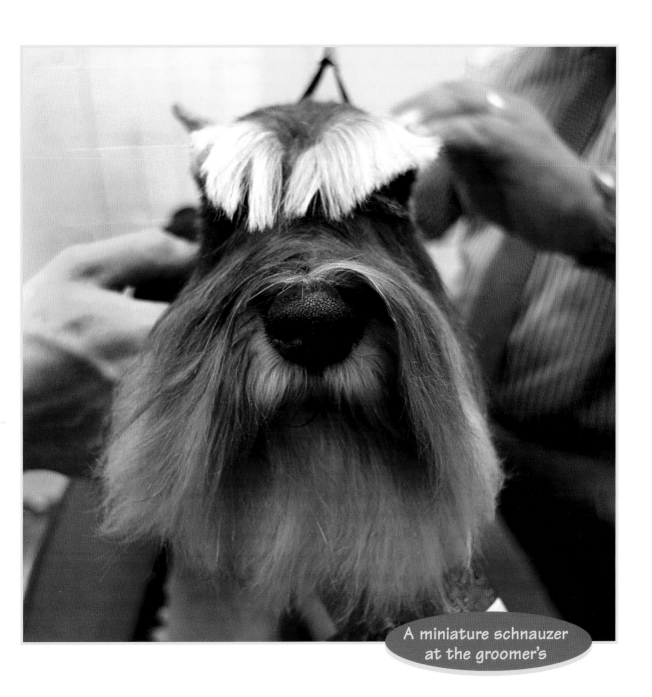

A miniature schnauzer at the groomer's

What About Training a Miniature Schnauzer?

Miniature schnauzers like learning and are usually smart, which is good, because if they are not well trained, they may become unruly.

A dog needs to learn who is boss. Thousands of years ago, when dogs were wild, they lived in groups called packs. Every dog pack had a lead dog that was the "boss." Dogs still need to know who the boss is, and it should be the person or people who will train it. A good trainer teaches a dog that he or she is the boss, but the trainer still treats the dog fairly and praises it often.

Consider taking your puppy to dog obedience school as soon as it is old enough—at about six months. This leaves little time for the dog to pick up bad habits. (Do not worry if your dog is older, however. Older dogs can be trained.) Obedience school can be a fun way to learn what training methods work best for your dog. Every dog should learn basic skills, such as how to walk on a leash, sit, stay, and come.

An obedient
miniature schnauzer

What Kinds of Exercise or Play Are Needed?

Exercise helps dogs to stay healthy and keeps them from getting bored—and a bored dog is more likely to get into trouble. Even though miniature schnauzers have a lot of energy, they also have a tendency to gain weight. They will probably not get enough exercise on their own just by running around the house or the yard. You should plan to take your dog on at least one walk a day.

Miniature schnauzers often love chasing a ball or playing Frisbee. And, if you are careful to train your dog and not to overdo it, it may also enjoy going jogging with you.

A miniature schnauzer
playing with a snowball

Do Miniature Schnauzers Like Doing Tricks?

Miniature schnauzers are known for being eager and easy to train, and they love attention, so they tend to enjoy performing tricks. Dog tricks might include barking on command or learning to bow. If you want to try to teach your dog tricks, begin with a simple one, such as rolling over or "shaking hands."

As with any animal training, the key to teaching your dog tricks is to speak the commands clearly and firmly, practice a lot, and use positive reinforcement *(REE ihn FAWRS muhnt).* Positive reinforcement means that when your dog does something good, you praise the animal, and perhaps give it a treat.

Once your dog has mastered some simpler tricks, you can try to teach it more difficult ones, such as fetching. You can even make up your own tricks.

Dogs need to practice their training skills often. It is better for a dog to practice for a brief time every day of the week than to have a longer training session once a week.

A miniature schnauzer
performing a trick

35

Should You Breed Your Miniature Schnauzer?

Most people should not breed their dogs, however fun it sounds to have cute puppies around. There are many more pets in the world than people who want to take them in. It is estimated that up to 8 million dogs and cats go into shelters in the United States every year, and only about half find homes. One out of four dogs in shelters is a purebred.

The most helpful thing you can do is to have your vet perform an operation on your dog that prevents it from being able to have puppies. This way, you do not make the problem of unwanted animals worse. Spaying prevents pregnancy in a female dog, and neutering makes a male dog permanently unable to father pups.

If you do decide to breed your miniature schnauzer, you will need to know how to care for the puppies. Have someone present who is experienced with dog births. Talk to your veterinarian about puppy foods and feeding methods.

A mother and her puppies

Are There Special Organizations for Miniature Schnauzer Owners?

In the United States, the main organization for people who love miniature schnauzers is the American Miniature Schnauzer Club. There are about 25 local branches of the club throughout the country. Similar organizations outside the United States include the Miniature Schnauzer Club of Canada and the Miniature Schnauzer Club, located in the United Kingdom.

The main goal of these clubs is to provide reliable information about miniature schnauzers. They can put breeders and dog owners in touch with each other and help people understand how best to take care of their dogs. Local clubs may also sponsor gatherings and events for miniature schnauzers and their owners. You can find out more about these organizations by visiting the Web sites listed on page 64.

A miniature schnauzer and its owner

How Do Miniature Schnauzers Help People?

Early in the history of the breed, miniature schnauzers helped their owners by controlling vermin and guarding their property. But today, most miniature schnauzers help by being friendly companions to the people they live with.

Some miniature schnauzers have a special job that allows them to help people. These dogs have been trained as therapy dogs. A therapy dog acts as a companion to sick or elderly people. These dogs might visit people in a hospital or nursing home. Since miniature schnauzers often have so much energy, you might not think that they would be good at visiting people who are sick or frail. Surprisingly, with their clever and playful personalities, these dogs are actually well suited for cheering up people. With the right training, their high energy is not a problem and they make good therapy dogs.

A loyal companion

What Are Some Other Terrier Breeds?

The American Kennel Club (AKC) sets the standards (accepted rules) for dog breeds in the United States and keeps track of pedigrees. It divides dog breeds into groups. The AKC places the miniature schnauzer into the terrier group. Other breeds in this group include Airedale *(AIR dayl)* terriers, Bedlington *(BEHD lihng tuhn)* terriers, cairn *(kairn)* terriers, fox terriers, Kerry blue terriers, Scottish terriers, and West Highland white terriers.

Organizations similar to the AKC group breeds differently. The Canadian Kennel Club (CKC) uses the same system as the United States and classes the miniature schnauzer and all the other dogs listed above as terriers. The Kennel Club (KC), the United Kingdom's purebred organization, and the Australian National Kennel Council (ANKC) place all the dogs listed above into the terrier group except for the miniature schnauzer. They classify the miniature schnauzer in the utility group.

A Scottish terrier

What Is an Airedale Terrier?

Airedale terriers are named for the place they were first bred—the valley, or dale, of Aire, in northern England.

Most breeds in the terrier group are small- or medium-sized dogs, but the Airedale is an exception. Nicknamed the "King of Terriers," the Airedale ideally is almost 2 feet (61 centimeters) tall at the shoulder, and some are as heavy as 60 pounds (27 kilograms).

Experts believe the Airedale was created by crossing two types of dogs. One was a black-and-tan dog called an Old English terrier. This breed of dog no longer exists. Still, something remains, as Airedales today are colored either black-and-tan or tan-and-"grizzle" (gray mixed with black). The second type of dog used to create the Airedale was a hound called the otterhound. The otterhound loves water and, as a result, Airedales are great swimmers.

Airedales are known for being dignified, alert, intelligent, and very loyal to their owners. They have a history of doing brave work, from hunting badgers, otters, and weasels to serving as watchdogs and police dogs.

An Airedale terrier

What Is a Bedlington Terrier?

The Bedlington terrier is a dog that looks like a lamb. It has soft, curly fur and a long face. Bedlingtons are a medium-sized terrier, ideally around 16 inches (40 centimeters) tall at the shoulder and weighing around 20 pounds (9 kilograms).

The Bedlington terrier is named for the small mining town in the north of England where it originated. Experts are not sure which dogs went into creating the Bedlington breed. The first dog that was called a Bedlington terrier was born in 1825. Bedlingtons were used to hunt badgers, and they were also very useful for ridding a mine of rats. A mine is a large hole in the ground made for digging out valuable materials from the earth.

Bedlingtons come in several colors. Many of them are off-white (which breeders refer to as "sandy"); gray (called "blue" by breeders); and light brown (called liver). Bedlingtons can also be sandy-and-tan, blue-and-tan, or liver-and-tan.

A Bedlington terrier

What Is a Smooth Fox Terrier?

The smooth fox terrier was created to chase foxes out of underground hiding places for hunters. It is a fairly small dog, ideally about 15 inches (38 centimeters) tall at the shoulder. It should weigh about 18 pounds (8 kilograms). Its legs are relatively long, though, so it can run through the woods and keep up with the other dogs used for fox hunting. The appearance of the breed has not changed much since it was first developed in the late 1700's in England.

The smooth fox terrier is white with patches of black, tan, or both black and tan. The smooth fox terrier and the wire fox terrier, another breed that has a coarser, longer coat, look quite a bit alike. They used to be considered one breed, but because their early ancestors are different, the American Kennel Club began considering them two different breeds in 1985.

A smooth fox terrier

49

What Is a West Highland White Terrier?

As its name reveals, the West Highland white terrier is a white dog that comes from the western part of the Highlands in Scotland. Some call the breed by its nickname, Westie. The Westie is related to cairn, Dandie Dinmont, Skye, and Scottish terriers—breeds that were also developed in Scotland.

Westies are low to the ground, with short legs to help them scramble under rocks and into holes. Ideally, a Westie is 10 to 11 inches (25 to 28 centimeters) tall at the shoulder. A dog of this breed should weigh from 13 to 19 pounds (6 to 9 kilograms).

The West Highland white terrier has a wiry coat about 2 inches (5 centimeters) long. The coat is made up of two layers of different textures: a coarse outer layer that resists dirt, and a soft, dense layer underneath that helps Westies stay dry if their adventures take them into a stream. Westies are famous for having a cheerful personality.

50

A West Highland
white terrier

What Is a Dog Show Like?

At dog shows, owners enter their pets in various competitions. Such shows are often sponsored by local chapters of organizations like the American Kennel Club or the Canadian Kennel Club.

Conformation is probably the best-known show event. In that event, a judge looks at the physical traits of a group of dogs from the same breed. The judge decides which dog is the best example of its breed. Winning dogs are awarded points. By winning enough points, a dog earns its championship.

Obedience trials are also popular events. At some types of obedience events, a dog may be asked to closely obey a number of commands, such as "heel," or "sit." As in a conformation show, points are awarded, and with enough points, the title of CD (companion dog) may be added behind the dog's registered name. At another type of obedience event, a dog may be judged on how well it retrieves or how well it can identify a certain scent. With enough points, the dog may earn the title of UD (utility dog). Often in obedience events, it is not necessary for the dogs that are competing to be purebred.

Miniature schnauzers
at a dog show

Are There Dangers to Dogs Around the Home?

Dogs cannot know what is safe around your house and what is not. People are responsible for keeping a pet out of danger.

Certain foods, such as chocolate, are poisonous to dogs (see page 24). A number of popular plants, like mums and English ivy, can also be poisonous. Do not allow your dog to eat or drink anything that could be dangerous or deadly. Follow this rule: If you don't know what it is or whether it's harmful, don't let your dog eat it, drink it, or chew on it.

When you leave home, you may need to put your dog in a dog crate. A dog crate is a large box made of metal wire or heavy plastic with air holes. Crates help dogs to feel more secure (unafraid), and they give a dog a safe place.

Never let your dog run loose outside of a fenced yard or off its leash. One of the biggest causes of death or injury for a pet is being hit by a car.

A miniature schnauzer
at home

What Are Some Common Signs of Illness?

Because dog breeds are created by matching parents with specific physical traits, and often dogs are matched from the same family, some breeds can be prone to special health problems.

Terriers are healthy dogs overall, perhaps because they were usually bred to be active, rather than to look pretty. Certain eye problems, such as glaucoma *(glaw KOH muh)* and cataracts, may trouble some kinds of terriers. Miniature schnauzers are at higher risk for diabetes *(DY uh BEE tihs)* than some other dogs. Diabetes is a disease that disrupts an animal's ability to use the sugars found in food.

The most common signs of illness in any dog are a change of behavior and loss of appetite. Any changes in a dog's physical appearance may also be a sign that it is not feeling well. Check your dog's skin, coat, and eyes, and stay alert to mood changes. Do not hesitate to call your veterinarian if you suspect something is wrong.

A tired miniature schnauzer

57

What Routine Veterinary Care Is Needed?

A dog should get a medical checkup once a year, even if nothing seems wrong. This is called preventive *(prih VEHN tihv)* care, because the idea is to prevent illness before it happens. The veterinarian will look at your dog's eyes, ears, and teeth, and feel its body for possible signs of illness.

Your dog may be due to have vaccinations (shots). A vaccine is a special medicine that protects people, dogs, and other animals from certain serious diseases. Your vet will also check your dog for parasites, such as fleas, ticks, and ear mites. These parasites can make your dog uncomfortable. They can also spread disease.

Find a veterinarian you like and keep going to that office, so the doctor gets to know your dog and has a complete medical record. This is not always possible, though. If you need to change veterinarians, ask for a copy of your pet's records to give the new doctor.

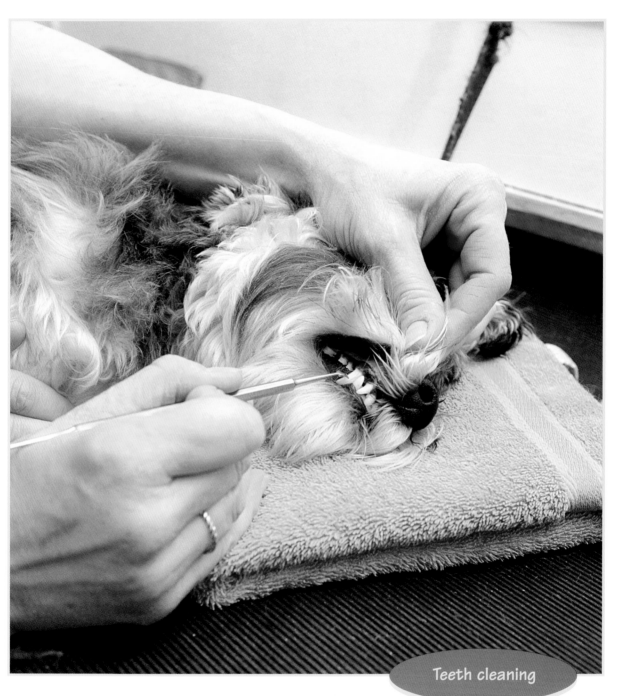

Teeth cleaning

59

What Are Your Responsibilities as an Owner?

When you get a dog, you take on responsibilities for the well-being of your pet. You agree to do everything possible to keep it healthy and happy. You provide such daily necessities as food, water, and exercise, as well as grooming and medical care as needed. If you take your dog to public areas, you make sure it behaves well and clean up its messes.

Perhaps the most significant responsibility that comes with dog ownership is the love and time you devote to your pet. Even if it has everything else it needs, a dog will not be happy if its family ignores it. It would rather play with you in the park than by itself in a fenced yard. There is nothing a dog likes more than giving and getting affection.

All dogs need exercise and companionship.

Terrier Fun Facts

→ In 1777, during the American Revolution, one of George Washington's soldiers found a dog—according to many reports, a fox terrier—wandering on the battlefield. The dog's collar identified its owner as William Howe, the British general leading the enemy army. As a dog lover himself, Washington knew Howe must be terribly worried, so he attached a note to the animal's collar and stopped the fighting long enough to return the dog.

→ During the 1880's, a Skye terrier named Bobby became famous in Scotland for his devotion to his owner. Bobby and his owner, John Gray, were always together. After John died in 1858, Bobby spent much of his time for the next 14 years sitting at his owner's grave. When Bobby died, he was buried near his master's grave.

→ The cairn terrier began in the Highlands and island regions of Scotland. The dog received its name because of its ability to dig under cairns (heaps of stones) to hunt rats and other animals. In the 1939 movie *The Wizard of Oz,* the part of Dorothy's dog, Toto, was played by a cairn terrier named Terry.

Glossary

allergy A reaction caused by something that would not ordinarily be harmful to humans, such as animal fur or dust.

ancestor An animal from which another animal is directly descended. Usually, *ancestor* is used to refer to an animal more removed than a parent or grandparent.

breed To produce animals by carefully selecting and mating them for certain traits. Also, a group of animals having the same type of ancestors.

breeder A person who breeds animals.

burrow A hole dug in the ground by an animal for shelter.

groom To take care of an animal, for example, by combing, brushing, or trimming its coat.

litter The young animals produced by an animal at one birthing.

neuter To operate on a male animal to make it unable to produce young.

pack A number of animals of the same kind hunting or living together. Also, a group of dogs kept together for hunting.

parasite An organism (living creature) that feeds on and lives on or in the body of another organism, often causing harm to the being on which it feeds.

pedigree A record of an animal's ancestors.

purebred An animal whose parents are known to have both belonged to one breed.

shed To throw off or hair, skin, fur, or other body covering.

spay To operate on a female animal to make it unable to have young.

trait A feature or characteristic particular to an animal or breed of animals.

vermin Animals that are considered by many to be troublesome or destructive.

Index (**Boldface** indicates a photo, map, or illustration.)

For more information about miniature schnauzers and other terriers, try these resources:

Books:
The Complete Dog Book for Kids by the American Kennel Club (Howell Book House, 1996)
Dogs by Bruce Fogle (DK Publishing, 2006)
The Terrier Breeds by Barbara J. Patten (Rourke, 1996)
The Terrier Handbook by Kerry V. Kern (Barron's Educational Series, 2005)

Web sites:
American Kennel Club
http://www.akc.org
Australian National Kennel Council
http://www.ankc.org.au/home/default.asp
The Canadian Kennel Club
http://www.ckc.ca/en/

The Kennel Club
http://www.thekennelclub.org.uk/
American Miniature Schnauzer Club
http://amsc.us/
American Miniature Schnauzer Club Rescue
http://amsc.us/index.php?option=com_content&task=view&id=25&Itemid=41
Miniature Schnauzer Club of Canada
http://www.mscc.ca/
The Miniature Schnauzer Club (United Kingdom)
http:/the-miniature-schnauzer-club.co.uk

Dog Classification

Scientists classify animals by placing them into groups. The animal kingdom is a group that contains all the world's animals. Phylum, class, order, and family are smaller groups. Each phylum contains many classes. A class contains orders, an order contains families, and a family contains genuses. One or more species belong to each genus. Each species has its own scientific name. Here is how the animals in this book fit into this system.

Animals with backbones and their relatives (Phylum Chordata)
Mammals (Class Mammalia)
Carnivores (Order Carnivora)

Dogs and their relatives (Family Canidae)

Domestic dog .... *Canis familiaris*

E
J   Janice

          Little Bear's New
C2   ML   Year's party

DATE DUE

JAN 5 1981			
JAN 3 1983			